GLASS BONES
AND
PAPER SKIN

AKSHARA GUPTA

BLUEROSE PUBLISHERS
India | U.K.

Copyright © Akshara Gupta 2025

All rights reserved by author. No part of this publication may be reproduced, stored in a retrieval system or transmitted in any form or by any means, electronic, mechanical, photocopying, recording or otherwise, without the prior permission of the author. Although every precaution has been taken to verify the accuracy of the information contained herein, the publisher assumes no responsibility for any errors or omissions. No liability is assumed for damages that may result from the use of information contained within.

BlueRose Publishers takes no responsibility for any damages, losses, or liabilities that may arise from the use or misuse of the information, products, or services provided in this publication.

For permissions requests or inquiries regarding this publication, please contact:

BLUEROSE PUBLISHERS
www.BlueRoseONE.com
info@bluerosepublishers.com
+91 8882 898 898
+4407342408967

ISBN: 978-93-7018-025-3

Cover design: Yash Singhal
Typesetting: Namrata Saini

First Edition: May 2025

Prologue

Foolish girl, why conquer a tale of woe?

Dedicated to my muses

07/09/2023 - 11/11/2024

Contents

1) Reverie 1
2) Gone 2
3) Locked 3
4) Strings of Illusion 4
5) Giving myself away 5
6) Not at all 6
7) Parted ways 7
8) Something did change 8
9) Somnolence 9
10) Tied 10
11) Shadows of Light 11
12) Blade marks 12
13) Wynorrific 13
14) To Be Loved is to Be Known 14
15) Good night 16
16) Unnoticed 17
17) The Man Under My Window 18
18) Finish 20
19) Done 21
20) Death 22
21) October promises 23
22) Broken 24
23) promise 26
24) Pages after Pages 27
25) Home 28
26) Romantica 29

27)	To the Monster Under My Bed	31
28)	Rose Garden	32
29)	Dying	33
30)	Synonyms	35
31)	2 hearts 1 lover	36
32)	Quiet	37
33)	In Remembrance of Thou	38
34)	Deal with the Devil	39
35)	Loving you	40
36)	Loving myself	42
37)	It Wasn't Ever Love	43
38)	An Asisines Death	45
39)	Peeling an Orange	46
40)	Mom and Dad	48
41)	Pretty or Not	49
42)	My Baby	50
43)	Ode to the Thunder	52
44)	Unrelenting Deluge	53
45)	Ugly	54
46)	Cease to Exist	56
47)	Quietude	57
48)	Fantasy	58
49)	Ruins	59
50)	Up close	60
51)	Fading hearts	61
52)	Loving you	62
53)	Unbreakable	63
54)	Pen to Paper	64
55)	The Hole	65

56) Mask 66
57) Music 67
58) His eyes 68
59) Unnamed 69
60) High note 70
61) Dandelions 72
62) Retaliation 73
63) Merged 74
64) All Good Things End (because of us) 76
65) Lost 77
66) To regret 78
67) Unlovable 79
68) Incomplete 81
69) Self-care 83
70) Once Was 84
71) You're rotting in my mind 85
72) to be an insect 86
73) Beauty 87
74) Unknown 88
75) Tongue Twister 89
76) Our end 90
77) Therapist 91
78) Regret 92
79) 5W's and 1H 93
80) Put your hand in mine 95
81) Fire, Flames, and Berries 96
82) Hopeless 97
83) No one 98
84) Grief 99

85) Corrupt 100
86) Remnants 101
87) Garnish of Gaia 102
88) Time 103
89) Changing 104
90) Who am I 105
91) Numb 107
92) Never Meant to Be 108
93) Ineffable 109
94) Words 110
95) Last 111
96) My Heart, a Sacred Temple; who I am 112
Haiku's 114

1) Reverie

You stand on the mountain
A pillar of your thoughts
and view the whole world
Where the good rests, and the bad rots
You discover a tapestry
of what makes you, you
You pull on a string
as it untangles
Glides to the ground like dew

2) Gone

the more I try to keep you in my arms
the more you slip away
and I grasp
to hold onto you
but I realize
I'm catching the empty air
and the wind you turned into.

3) Locked

You gave me your heart
But kept the key
So I stand here, trying to enter
As behind the door
you laugh at my misery.

4) Strings of Illusion

Often, I feel as if
I am a toy
and you the puppeteer
Pulling on my strings
brings you joy
While my worn-out state
only brings me tears.

5) Giving myself away

I cut off my eyes
when I realized you couldn't see
Yet even after wearing them
you never looked at me

you were never happy
so, I gave you my smile
and sat there, sullen
Hoping you'd grin at me once in a while

You needed to reach further ahead
so tearing off my limbs was a must
but you snatched them and ran away
leaving me alone, watching you in the dust.

6) Not at all

if you love me
for what I look like
then it's only your eyes
in love with what they see

if you love me
for my words
then it's only your ears
in love with what they hear

if you love me
for my skin
then it's only your body
in love with what it touches, not from what it does within

if you love me
for my heart
      soul
      mind
      every flaw
then it's you
in love with me whole
in love with me with all.

7) Parted ways

The worst feeling in the world
is losing a friends
for unlike a temporary lover
your heart you had lent
And even if you believe it's in the past
or it doesn't hurt anymore
They ran away with your memories
leaving you bruised and sore

8) Something did change

mornings with you
made me love the sunshine
nights with you
made me love each star

after you left
nothing had changed

except the sun being too irritatingly bright
and the once divine stars
now littering the sky

9) Somnolence

I've been exhausted all week
Because after you stopped texting goodnight
I stopped sleeping

> I try to fondle myself to sleep
> Stroke my hair like you once did
> But as I begin to drift off
> Your touch abandons my body

And I'm up again.

10) Tied

Sometimes I wish that
our veins were tied together
So, you'd never be able to
leave me
They'd take
red blood
to each of our hearts
Mixing in a way
That it won't ever separate

11) Shadows of Light

My eyes are open
But I cannot see
Darkness above me
Crushes me with its weight
Down, down
Till only shards remain

12) Blade marks

I begin with peace, hoping to end there
I don't want to depart a violent corpse

I don't want to depart a violent corpse
corrupt with blade marks that'd shock a soldier

some of the marks depict a portrait of my growth
some of them depict my disgust
even paint can't cover them

paint could cover yours
wrath and fear disguised plain
under a mask of sheet
what is the reason. for your violence?

here is a reason for mine:
I feel deeply

I feel lightly
in the faraway dream
where I am a river

in the dream where I am a river
I carry your trash
but I flow to vast corners
I flow with peace

I hope to end there.

12 | Akshara Gupta

13) Wynorrific

Laying on the couch
Her hand grasped the pen
Incessant thoughts
She scribbles relentlessly, when
Her mind runs too fast
Her hands start to shake
She screams at herself
Maybe it's time for a break
But her mind doesn't let go
The pen pierces her palm
A journey to find solace
Has robbed her of calm

14) To Be Loved is to Be Known

I don't want half hearted
almost
kind of
maybe not
Mixed signals
making me rethink every thought
'Almost brought you those flowers
almost gave you a call
almost came to see you
almost gave you my all'
'I slept early
that's why I didn't drop a single text'
(Although he's probably choosing which girl to talk to
next)
'I'm not the type of guy
who'll sit at home trying to make flowers from paper
(Too cool for that; he'll probably just say see you later)
I don't want a guy
who I'll tell people I like
and they'll ask why
What's so appealing about his
nonchalant nature
uncaring act
effortless attitude
Why do only these guys you attract?

'I left a letter on your desk
Can I see you later today
I know you have your game,
can I come watch you play?'
'I brought you your favorite tulips
Please don't go out of my sight
Just stay on the call for a while more
Please, please read me the poetry you write?'
'Can I hold your hand
make your world calm
as I listen to every word you say
trace circles around your palm'
(You make me feel whole
you make me feel complete
you've fixed pieces of my heart
that I was sure would never meet)

I don't want half hearted
insecure
doesn't care about anything I do
I don't want half hearted
and that's why I chose to love you.

15) Good night

today I let my heartbeat
cradle me to sleep
hoping that as it sang its lullaby
I would feel my blood
rushing through my veins
reminding me
I am alive

16) Unnoticed

everyone praises the poetry
but never the poet
admires the art
never the artist
and that makes me think
I could give my all
pour out my heart and soul
piece by piece
but I'd still stay hidden behind my work
no one cares to look further
I stuck a needle in my vein
the dark red blood filling up the tube
layer by layer
and I wrote my pain with its color
staining my hands
yet they only look at the words
uncaring to look deeper
as somewhere near
my drained body lies on the floor

17) The Man Under My Window

There's a man under my window
and every time I look at him
he asks me to jump

I try to tell my mom
But all she does is laugh
and tells me to get out of my head
she shuts the blinds
and the curtains stained red

I see the looks people give me
as they walk past
They call me crazy
I hope this feeling doesn't last

The man under my window
just won't let me go
He keeps begging
and ive always been a people pleaser

I took a ladder
Stood up on the ledge
And I take a step forward
I fall

Down, down, down
Or maybe I don't

I don't know what's real anymore

18) Finish

I need to know how to stop
loving you
pouring myself into your broken vase
as my efforts to fill you up
diminish with me
emptying myself
as your vase remains empty
and spills me on the grubby floor

19) Done

I think I held onto you too tightly
What I thought was my loving hands on your skin
Were my sharp nails digging into your flesh
What I thought was my body hugging yours
Absorbing all the love within
Was really my frame gripping you in a way
That left you unable to move
as I slowly strangled every inch of you

I'm sorry if I held onto you too tight
And caused you to burst
Into tiny pieces

20) Death

Loving someone is the best medicine, they say
So why am I losing breath
As my heart caves in
My lungs fill with poison
Choking to death

21) October promises

Dear October,
you must be
my disloyal lover
who snuck from the warm sheets
we both lay in
and left me behind
in the cold, cruel
darkness

you wandered away
into the lonely night
as I slept, unknowing
dreaming of our future together
what we would do
the things we would be
reminding myself
that no matter what it holds
I have you
and you have me

Dear October
before you bade me your silent goodbye
did you promise
to visit me again?

another lie
on your frozen lips

22) Broken

Always the artist
never the muse
always the considerate
whose love was just being used
always the storyteller
never the tale
always the character
never explained in detail
What if rather than the composer
I wanted to be the melody instead
not the girl who's lost her mind
and is rotting in her own head
What if instead of the dreamer
I wanted to be the dream
rather than a shadow
a girl just wanting to be seen

Born to be the lead
forced to be just the side character instead
born to be a novel
forced to be a bunch of words unread
born to live with hope
forced to always be let down instead
born with big aspirations
forced to walk with them dead

Born to be loved
but always the lover
who gives out her heart
yet it is still to be discovered.

23) promise

you said you loved me
yet you did
nothing
to make me stay
I told you I'd walk out
and you just
moved out of my way

I told you id gotten
my heart broken once before
you promised that won't happen
and now, it's all sore

again

24) Pages after Pages

It's hard to write about your eyes
not only because they look like gems
they have oceans vast and deep
what if I drown in them?
Your hair, thick and curly
that I could fill pages about
what if I get lost in the locks
and can't find my way out?
For your smile, I have a lot to say
Bright and blinding
melts my worries away
The way you talk
How you're so empathetic and kind
The way you act
The way you read my mind
About your charisma
I can fill up a hundred pages or more
 Your beauty and nature
yet there is so much left to explore
So I'll grab a pen and paper
and write bit my bit
even though I realize
I kind of already just did

25) Home

You stand on my porch
wet and shaking
gasping for breath
and ask if you can stay
you need time away
from the door slamming
glass throwing
screaming and yelling
I welcome you in
and tell you this
is your new home
I let you stay for
as long as you like
I just didn't expect
after all these years
you wouldn't leave
though I have not seen you in a while
you stayed and
made a home
in my heart

26) Romantica

She calls herself a hopeless romantic
one who always looks at love
but love never looks her way
she doesn't really have a list
of the qualities her man should have
all he needs to do
is love her back
swipe left, swipe right
she goes out to meet people
a phone full of heartbreaking messages
and apologies
'It comes when you stop searching', they tell her
But how can she stop searching
when all she ever does is
wonder if it awaits somewhere near?
She has started doubting herself
maybe she isn't pretty enough
or interesting
maybe they just find her boring
a shadow bustling around
while everyone falls in love
she falls apart
breaking herself
just to be loved

She calls herself a hopeless romantic

one who always looks at love
but love never looks her way

27) To the Monster Under My Bed

I was never scared of you
never cried to my parents like other friends
didn't sleep with the lights on to keep you away
Never knew I'd be upset when our time would end
You used to hide under my bed
while above you, lonely me would lay
You kept still and silent
as I'd tell you all about my day
I began to trust you
You never did judge
I asked you to show me you were there
A sound, move, nudge?
I began to grow tired
of the one-sided conversation we had
Were you actually hiding there?
The lack of response made me mad
Monster, you were my only friend
Heard me out when no one did
So why did you run when I needed you the most
Disappeared and hid

28) Rose Garden

Entering the rose garden
above the valley
Climbing up the fragments of rocks
through the uncut, tall grass
You to sit within the rose petals
merged with their glamour
It would be wrong to say you chose to do this
because you don't make decisions
Decisions make you
like a tulip, petal by petal
covers each inch of you
keeps you hiding in its warmth
either poisons your mind
or fills it with love
It makes you sit in the rose garden
buried under haywire grass and
the strange smell of yesterday's dew

29) Dying

when you pluck a flower from a plant she dies
even if you keep her in a beautiful vase
where the sun can always be seen shining
or there is plenty of water to drink
she still dies

you snatched her from the place
her heart belonged to
and kept her stored in a container
like a lifeless statue
just for yourself

her roots are bare
all her buried insecurities
displayed in bright light
visible for everyone to judge and mock
as they stare at them
instead of her petals

you appear to take care of her
water her daily
but all you have done is
stolen a beautiful thing for yourself
not caring that you are killing her

a week passes by
you notice the flower wilting in its cage
caving into her torture
'it looks ugly', you decide
and throw her out

all that is left of her
are a few dried petals
a reminder of who she once was
before he came and ruined her

maybe in another universe
he let the flower be
and she blossomed,
like a rainbow emerging in spring

perhaps, beauty is meant to be seen, not touched

30) Synonyms

The opposite if suicide is belonging
a collection of books lined up on the shelf-

A bunch of books littering the floor
filled with pointless poetry that you step on

Poetry may be pointless, but it gives you hope
something the fear let you keep

The fear corrupting your mind
drove you past bookshelves to windows

To windows from bookshelves
The opposite of suicide is belonging.

31)   2 hearts 1 lover

I broke my own heart fixing yours
breaking apart it's pieces
and trying to fix them into your gaps
scratching off my bright red
to paint color into you
I pulled off my uneven edges
to refine yours
and then, as your heart became whole
and mine fell apart
I realized that while chasing the idea of you loving me
I left my ability to love far behind

32) Quiet

I wasn't always this quiet
I used to have stories to tell
but when I realized no one would really listen
I locked them up instead
I am like a library
full of tales untold
if a few words would to be exchanged
my pages would unfold
I wasn't always this quiet
I always had something to say
now every word, phrase, thought
in an abandoned library they lay

so don't call me quiet
if you cared for my words, they would flow out my mouth
don't call me quiet
if you choose to mute me out

33) In Remembrance of Thou

My bed feels empty
The blanket does no justice to your warmth
I find it hard to believe
That I lost you over my swarth

The flowers do not smell so fresh
Calm breeze now attacks my face
My body craves your soothing caress
The rain screams at my colossal mistake

I loathe myself for letting you go
You were my forever, we both knew
So I sit alone, yelling 3 words of sorrow
I miss you.

34) Deal with the Devil

The infant sound asleep in its cot-
the mother watches on teary eyed
a soul for a soul is what the devil sought
no matter who lived for who died

35) Loving you

I'm in love with you
I swear that's not a lie
I'm completely in love with you
you might wonder why

I don't love you how love now works
Where it happens for a bit then it'll go
Where it's onto the next in seconds
Where it's made of make promises or so

I love you like I always need to be next to you
I always need to hear what you'd say
I love you like I can never get tired of you
Like without you, I can't imagine my day

I'm in love with you
I mean, what did you expect?
You might wonder why
Is it your good looks, or intellect?
But it's for your heart
so kind, too pure
I'm a sick woman
you're my only cure
For the way you're always ready to help
those who are in need
because you genuinely want to

not for the sake of doing a good deed

For the way you always hear me out
I know you'll never judge
The way you forgive and forget
You aren't one to hold a grudge

For the way you always welcome life
and everything it gives
the way you dream of our future
and the way we'll live

I love you
I swear that's not a lie
I'm completely in love with you
These are a few reasons why

36) Loving myself

I'm worthless
and you can never make me believe that
I'm not a mess
I'm well aware
that I have an ugly soul
and nothing can convince me
my heart isn't an empty hole
it's true that
I don't belong
you lie when you say
that I'm not wrong
you try to tell me
I don't mean a lot
so ill never be convinced
I'm not born to simply rot

Now read this backwards

37) It Wasn't Ever Love

Can it be heartbreak, if it was never really love?
to me, you were like a warm summer afternoon
to you, I was the painful heat shining from above
You felt like leaping into the ice pool
the cool water soothing the sides of my hot face
To you, I was the hungry wasp buzzing in circles
something you'd want to erase

There had come a time
when I realized you preferred the winter snowfall instead
so, I dropped my sunglasses,
left behind my hat
and wore the thick scarf painted red

You saw me in my scarf
and my thick fur fleece
yet u didn't even spare me a glance
making my heart break piece by piece

can it be heartbreak, if it was never really love?
I sit on your doorstep
as snowflakes fall heavily like rain
I'm sick of the winter
my heart is in pain

I wish I had stayed in summer

38) An Asisines Death

The huntress meets the vagrant
behind the citadel
concealed from malevolence
their optics clash all too well
Vermillion and tantalizing
merge with his angelic blue
Oh, imprudent one
how besotted can you be?
The huntress waits, blade at hand
Inamorato will perish with agony

39) Peeling an Orange

Late at night and we were sitting in my kitchen
I told you I loved oranges
but I liked the act of peeling them more than eating them
The feeling of love and attention
merged within each cut
was better than its sweet taste
I offered to peel you one
but you could do it yourself, you claimed
and took a knife from the cupboard as I brought the
orange and gave it to you
you stabbed the fruit
piercing its soft skin
butchering its flesh
as its juice spurted out
staining the floor and my cushions
denting the cutting board
Its peel flew around
and landed in corners
where my mop doesn't reach
You laugh and I hear you say
it's too much work
you'd rather eat some grapes
I stare at you with bewilderment
as my heart breaks apart into tiny fragments
I think about the day
I'll become too much work for you

I have many layers you'll need to peel
and you'll be too tired
you'll go for someone with less layers to peel apart
someone who doesn't create a
mess of your kitchen
someone who's easier

I would peel a hundred oranges for you
and you'd just get tired of peeling me one

40) Mom and Dad

My mother's stress
is leaking into my chest
When she looks into my eyes
brown eyes that she gave me
I wonder if she knows
how her worry has started to
make its home in my heart
I've got my father's nose
and his smile
and his ability to lie
about the littlest of things
so, I'm sorry
for the time I said
I hadn't seen your 7 missed calls
because I was studying
I lied
I watched my phone ring
I had already made the excuse
I swear I wouldn't have lied if I could.

41) Pretty or Not

What type *pretty* are you?
standard pretty, model pretty, popular pretty
deer, squirrel, fox
the list goes on
you're either one of these or just not
'Doe eyes or siren eyes?', they ask
and if your eyes take any other shape
your face is out of trend
natural versus glam
symmetrical versus asymmetrical
oval face versus diamond face
it's exhausting
because being beautiful just by being you isn't enough
for beauty standards come and change
as your beauty will expire
if you don't fit in a category
are you even pretty?
welcome to being a woman in the 21st century
where toxic strangers on the internet decide how you
should see yourself

42) My Baby

I miss my baby
I miss her hands as big as my finger
the soft skin I would trace
she had eyes, big and blue
for her smile, mountains I could chase
I used to work from 5 in the morning
till 7 in the evening
she'd come kiss my forehead
and leave torn pieces of paper
which said she loves me
I miss receiving those notes
we'd run in the garden
she loved to play catch
she'd wait for me to hold her
and throw her up in the air
and catch her into my arms
she knows I won't let her fall
she'd sleep with a teddy
who she called bear
as she drifted off
she would hold him tight
just like I would do her
we played dress up
I made her wear a pink dress
and she wore a tiara on her head
she'd try to walk in my heels

laughing
My little Cinderella
I miss sitting in my armchair
reading stories
she told me she felt sad for the 3 piggies
she cried
I told her about the time she used to be in my belly
as I would caress it over and over
trying to feel a kick
the slightest feel
she would laugh

'I miss my baby'
I think
as I lie on the bed
my hands on my stomach
I hope I'll be there with her tomorrow night.

43) Ode to the Thunder

The night is dark, in taciturnity I lay
Neither a star visible nor the moon's ray
Not once am I blessed with the valour to open an eye
but have lain still, convict to the thunder's cries

Thunder, you are the nefariouses nightmare
for you seize him without a care
hence it is my humble request
to take the covetous and let the blameless rest.

44) Unrelenting Deluge

The rain pours down heavily
shows no mercy
to the poor homeless getting drenched
or to the ones laying on the street dead

Oh pluie! verse tes larmes
Laisse la ville voir tes peurs
Venge- toi de ceux qui t'ont fait du mal
Jusqu'a ce que tu sois en paix et calme.

45) Ugly

Olivia was 8 when her teacher asked her class to draw something ugly
and when she gave in her work
her teacher looked stumped to find a poorly drawn scribble of herself
'Do you think you are ugly'?
she asks Olivia after making her wait after class
Her silence was more of an answer than what her words would have been
'Why?' the teacher asks desperate for a glimpse into the child's mind
Olivia knew her words would fail her yet again, so she did what she knew best
She brought out an ashen paper and drew a line
she broke the led but that didn't stop her from drawing
when she was done, the teacher had a look on her face, she decided
but she couldn't choose whether it was fear, confusion or sympathy
the teacher's eyes stayed glued to the picture
a stick figure with black wings on one end
one with white horns on another
the teacher didn't understand, Olivia knew
no one can understand
'It's my mind' her feeble voice tries to explain

The angel sat on one side, inviting her into her black feathers
bad decisions disguised as pure
The devil with white horns
trying to act guiltless
even though it's wired to be depraved
Olivia didn't know the lesser of two evils
she was ugly, inside and out
No one would never understand

Olivia filled the silence by grabbing the sheet and broken pencil and heading out the door.

46) Cease to Exist

Sometimes I wish I could just close my eyes
and make you disappear
because rather than listening to your lies
I could just pretend like you aren't here

47) Quietude

They say silence screams the loudest
I didn't believe them until
I asked if you ever did truly love me
and you responded without words

48) Fantasy

I could spend hours daydreaming
of the kind of woman I will grow to be
when time does its magic
Slowly changing everything along with me

When I am carefree in my twenties
Paying no heed to what others have to say
Fulfilling my younger, timid self's ambitions
Dancing through life's ways

Or when I find myself nearing forties
An eminent, thriving lady
Doing all that they said she never could
Watching as time starts acting shady

And then I'll be thrown into my sixties
as my body slows, and wrinkles appear
Reminiscing about my childhood antics
as I feel the time to leave near

49) Ruins

I often go outside
and try to breathe in some fresh air
but instead of calm and tonic
I smell the stench of ruin and massacre

50) Up close

My eyes can't see
very well
But that's okay
because all
I ever want to look at
is you

51) Fading hearts

You watch from a distance
as I look into his eyes
He takes my hands in his
making goosebumps rise
I still glance back at you
Only for you to flash a half smile
Your teary eyes holding onto our memories
as we pull on the string with all our secrets and lies

52) Loving you

How do you expect me to forgive and forget
after you snatched my heart from my body
and lit it on fire with your cigarette

> *Ashamed*
> *Im so ashamed how*
> *you could light me on fire*
> *and I'd still worry*
> *if the flames came near you*

53) Unbreakable

There are chains around my legs
that pull me back when I try to move
ripped into my flesh
dented my skin
so, I try to improve
I work twice as hard
I do what they say
yet the painful chains
won't go away

54) Pen to Paper

My mind is filled with thoughts
it never gets a rest
I try to write some down
but most go unsaid
I know its unfair
to expect everyone to understand me
when I hide everything about myself
for no one to see.

55) The Hole

It's been a couple years
since ive been running through this hole
its deep underground
so, no one knows
where I have been stuck, trying to escape
my legs always failing me
leaving me trapped in this cave
It's been a couple years
that's why I'm shocked to see
the end of the hole, leading me to the sky
where light awaits me
As I climb up
I whisper a goodbye to this hole
leaving behind my helpless nights
I can finally free my soul

56) Mask

I wonder if you'll still like me
when I pull down my mask
my true self revealed
would you still see my charm?
when my true face is shown
past mistakes and all
I hope that you'll still like me
as much as when the mask was on.

57) Music

Your mouth spews some words
but I don't understand them
for by the time they have reached my ears
they transformed into a melody
a symphony, of sorts

58) His eyes

The sun is too bright
always blinding me
so instead, I look into your eyes
and get all the light I'll ever need

59) Unnamed

I think I'm so used to living with screaming that calm makes my ears bleed.

60) High note

You say you're broken
I say you're wrong
you're actually a sweet melody
my favorite song

The one that's always stuck in my had
and I can't get it out of my mind
I listen to it for hours
the second it ends, I rewind

I love the tune
I've memorized each beat
I know every line
like a book, its lyrics I read

On the radio, a vinyl
a C.D or cassette
wherever I can find it
on listening to it, my heart is set

Stuck in my heart, in my mind
in my blood, in my veins
in my arms, in my legs
Am I going insane?

You say you're broken
I say you're wrong
you're actually a sweet melody
my favorite song

*you're all I want to listen to *

61) Dandelions

Entangled between the muck and the wilting grass
in the forest unseen
stands a dandelion, tall and inviting
Serene

I sit on my knees, ignoring the pricking grass
my rough hands caress its stem so smooth
as I gently blow, its feathers shiver and break apart
flying up in the sky, to their own truth

They fly up high
stoop down low
fight strong winds
but never touch the ground below

The dandelion sits in silence
watching its white feathers glide through the sky
as they go to find their own purpose
fly, and fly

62) Retaliation

I stand in the rain
Pouring down with ire
Lighting the world on fire
Yet the hurt in our heart remains

The city lies in disarray
Tears and aguish fill the crowd
The stillness is loud
As they clouds have their way

Throwing resentment towards humanity
For the mess we have made
Naïve nature we betrayed
Showers us with its brutality.

63) Merged

What's your favorite color?
Your favorite season to see
What kind of people do you like
and by any chance, does it describe me?

What kind of books do you read
novels, fiction... something along those lines?
have you read poetry?
do you (maybe) like mine?

What movies do you watch
a comedy, thriller, or blockbuster
I honestly don't care
because what you like if what I prefer
Rock, pop, jazz
What type of music do you like to hear
mines pretty obvious-
 your voice next to my ear

What's your favorite day of the week
Best date in the year?
I don't need to explain mine;
every single day that you're here

What are u fonder of;
the mountains or the beach

no need to ask me
as being a beach person, for you the highest mountains id reach

what IS your favorite color
please say its either pink or blue
because if I have every part of you
I want you to have a part of me too.

64) All Good Things End
(because of us)

Rome wasn't built in a day
but it burnt down
in a couple of hours
and its ashes
spread across the land
a faint reminder
of what the place once was
as they stand on top of it
with lit matches
and cigarettes that they drop
burning to crisps in its flame

65) Lost

Being a second choice
Is like being clothes too old to be worn
Kept in the closet, but never chosen
A dirty secret never shown

66) To regret

I can't undo
what I've done
I can't walk back the track
I've already run
I can't pick up the water
that's already been spilled
I can't save your heart
that's already been killed

I will always live with regret
you will always live with the pain that you can't forget.

67) Unlovable

I could be unlovable
or I could just be scared
a world filled with people
and I'm just not prepared
I could be unlovable
or maybe trusting someone is hard
we're in a game of poker
I can't have you seeing my every card
I could be unlovable
or I just be tired
searching again and again
who's honest and who's a liar
I could be unlovable
or I could be a book
full of poetry and paragraphs
that no one understood
Maybe I'm not unlovable
and it's not me, the problems you
I'm a heavy rainfall
and you're a single drop, or two
Maybe I'm not unlovable
I'm just more than what you deserve
your actions are weak
compared to your strong words
Maybe I'm not unlovable
and the universe is giving me a chance

to show me how much I'm worth
while you aren't even worth a glance

Maybe I'm not unlovable
I'm just too lovable for you.

68) Incomplete

It could have been great
I'm an artist with a
blank canvas in front of me
clean brushes and fresh paint
I remember all the strokes
I know what to do
but my hands seem stuck on the brush
unable to move
I could have made anything
a portrait, landscape...
but my mind appears to be blank.
like it's looking for an escape
No, no I'm not lazy
or looking for an excuse
in a race full of esteemed artists
the last thing I want to do is lose
I throw some paint on the canvas
why won't it stain?
it pools on the floor, around my legs
all my efforts in bloody vain
tears cloud my vision
now I can't see a thing
as everything becomes blurry and plain
like the canvas; my incomplete painting

with the brush in my hand

and the canvas in my eyes
I finish my 'great' painting
made with tears and lies.

69) Self-care

You might need your medicine. Me?
I've got my long, brown hair
I scrub the ends with
ice cold water
and braid it loose
you're my antihero
my patient daughter
I tell her, as she complains and grumbles
behind my ears
And later at night
I gently untangle my rope
and comb through the edges
Your fingers, like dew
through each strand of mine
I hear her say
As she rests herself
upon my slacken shoulders.

70) Once Was

I wash my face in the basin
and when I look up
the girl in the mirror
is no longer me
she is younger
louder, carefree
I watch her run through the grass
past the birds in the sky
to her friends on the swings
in her pink flower dress
and matching tights
she gets her feet of the ground
and tries to touch the clouds.

I wipe my face and go back to sleep.

71) You're rotting in my mind

I won't say I miss you
but my heart races when someone mentions your name
my ears stand up, trying to hear what they say
You probably don't waste a single second thinking about me
but my mind has a corner
where you always sit
you're plastered all around its walls
I've tried to pluck you out but
you just won't fall
it's embarrassing to admit
because you did me so wrong
never once apologized
and it's been so long
While you live on in peace
I want you to know
there's a replica of you stuck inside of me
rotting to its core.

72) to be an insect

lately, I have been feeling like a fly
trapped in those insect killers
my body being electrocuted
but I can do nothing except
wait for my death.

73) Beauty

you stab me with your knife
and yet all I notice
is the way your almond eyes glisten
and freckles litter your cheeks
how your pink lips quiver

I am grateful
this is my last memory

74) Unknown

I look into the mirror
and see my eyes
they were once bright and yellow
like the sun
now they're black
like tar
my lips
sealed shut
my face
looks distorted
I can't recognize myself
scrub, scrub, scrub
I rub the soap
everywhere
'Maybe something will change'
but nothing does
who is this?
standing in the mirror
pretending to be me
who is this?
I don't know

75) Tongue Twister

Do you ever pause and think
about the things you say
before your tongue lashes out
shoving everything in its way

Have you ever considered
how your words might destroy
what I see in myself
does my pain bring you joy?

And if someday
your comments morph my worth
your words become my mirror
leaving every part of me hurt

I just want you to know
your words may taint my skin
but they'll never reach my soul.

76) Our end

I'm writing our last chapter
but I don't know how it ends
but one thing I do know
is that I'll never start writing it again
You knew I was a good writer
I could write our pages without a break
I guess I forgot to understand
how much of my love you could take
I wanted to rewrite the beginning
give myself some hope
then I realized that trying to change the past
was tougher than strangling myself with a rope
While I try to fight for our love
no matter what I say
I can't ignore the fact that
for you it's just like another day
I really want to stop here
put the full stop where I last paused
but my mind is searching for any reason to write
do you realize how much suffering you have caused?
So, my pen stands there
stuck between moving on or not
it doesn't blame you for our end
it blames all the love I sought.

77) Therapist

I am not someone's cure
fixing them when they desire
medicine they can always use
and I am the supplier

My mind is not made to be filled
with troubles of your own
when my own thoughts can't fit
and I remain unknown.

78) Regret

I look down at my hands
they're a bloody mess
my nails hide scraps of my skin
my fingertips hold its flesh

my arm lies bare
the ripped skin only shows
where my pain glides in
and regret flows

I look down at my hands
is this what they were meant to do?
replaces my shining yellow
with a dull shade of blue

and as I write this
my hands seem to shake
as if they were apologizing
for their daily mistake.

79) 5W's and 1H

I'm starting to believe
that our parents were right
when they told us
all along
the phone was the problem
Because how did
loving myself for who I am
turn into my worth
depending on what comments on my posts say
Spending hours to click a picture
with the right angle
for another's eyes
I wonder when
running through fresh flowers
on grass with dew
changed inro
endless scrolling on Instagram
losing track of time
And where did those friend
who I used to meet everyday
disappear behind a screen
the most we talk now
being a 'hi' on text
I ask why
gazing at my beauty in the mirror
transformed into begging to look like

someone else
as I don't let anyone see me
for who I am
desperately trying to change my identity
I question who
is happy
after being chained behind a device
losing track of themselves
I wonder what
my world would have been like
if I had listened to my parents
and left the phone
my individuality
unconsumed by
fake personas and
expectations.

80) Put your hand in mine

I remember how your hand felt
entangles with mine
the calmness of tracing your fingers
memorizing each dot and line
I remember the euphoria
of knowing I was loved
the anxiety of never wanting to let go
till I was to be welcomed above
I remember how your hand felt
and the comfort it brought
as I watch it lay in someone else's
slowly dies and rots.

81) Fire, Flames, and Berries

I am burning
Fire so bright, its blinding
wraps itself around me
like a blanket
worn on winter mornings
I am burning
my flesh seems to melt
my body is a candle
my skin is wax
I am burning
the fire finally reaches my heart
and all I think of is
I hope my ashes smell like
(pink) berries.

82) Hopeless

In my mind
stands a cliff
old and abandoned
I don't know what's below it
I maintain my distance
I usually stay away
from whatever horrors under
would silently lay
but one day I ran too close
I was just trying to have fun
I slipped down
down, down, down
below, like a piece of meat
thrown to a pack of lions
I lay there, unsure
waiting for a rope
the hope only lasted a week.
So I lay there
no way back up
I just lay
still.

83) No one

I'd been drowning in the ocean for months
waiting for someone in a boat
to come rescue me
but soon
I decided to swim back myself
I realized
I could swim this entire time
All I needed was to
set my eyes on the shore

84) Grief

In the somber depths of sorrows embrace
lies my preserved refuge
forgetting the whispers of solace
for our love you refused

Desolate, as I sit and recall
how I thought our bond could move mountains itself
but how can I grieve us when we didn't exist?
I finally grieve myself.

85) Corrupt

I stand in the shower
as the water strikes my face
icy and raw
making my heart race
It flows down my body
slowly, as if it were in pain
sliding down all my bumps and curves
alas all my efforts, in vain
For I am still the same woman I was
sad and impure
and all the long showers
will boon me no cure

86) Remnants

My eyes soulless
holding no hope
as I stare at the mirror
it pulls me in with its rope

My hollow heart
with nothing to see
what once held care and affection
leaves me, with nothing to be

My hands reach out to touch my face
the cold, hard flesh
pale and sick
an unwanted mess

I pull at my hair
has it always been this short?
pain hits my scalp
as I stare at it rot

My eyes, again, dead for everyone to see
but only I stand here
to watch them well with tears
glide down with agony.

87) Garnish of Gaia

The fronds on the tree dance with the gale
as it shrieks in agony and wails
the flowers, green and awaiting to be plucked
bees search for nectar to feast and suck

Nature, how do we repay you?
if only they could open their eyes and see
how you offer us your bones and blood
in the form of dew and mud.

88) Time

A conjurer, performing tricks left and right
shows its charm when we least expect
does it do this out of excitement or spite?
we just know of its effects

It will come to you when you are most joyous
and leave when you feel worse
it's only purpose is to destroy us
using its powerful curse

Oh time, a monster in disguise
you find joy in ending us quick
fooling us with your beautiful lies,
you truly are sick.

89) Changing

Doesn't it bother you
knowing how much you've changed
since the last couple years
nothing remains the same
Do you scroll through your camera roll
see the weird faces you made
the type of people you hung out with
who you'd now call strange
The music you listned to
why, you have no clue
The hobbies you loved
which now bore you
The way you used to talk
The way you used to act
The way you used to think
There is nothing same about you at all
Doesn't it bother you
knowing how much you've changed
and being aware that in a few years
you'll wonder this again.

90) Who am I

you look under the bed
lying on your knees
you pull apart the curtains
search through every crease
in every cupboard
inside each bag
on every table
under each rag
soon your mother sees
you tear apart her house
she asks what you are doing
'searching for who I am' you reply
and miss the look on her face

you search on google
read every book
yet the answer still hasn't found you
no matter where you look

your mother looks concerned
a tear falls out of her eye
as she stares at you mess the house
muttering 'who am I?'

you now know who created electricity
and how the earth was made

you can identify each star in the sky
you know every dinosaur's name

        but you still don't know
        who you are.

91) Numb

My heart beats without fire
my mind races without thoughts
my legs move with no rhythm
my arms lay still and rot

my mouth spits some words
boring and plain
they don't go through my ears
spoken in vain

I pinch and poke myself
leaving only bruises around
the ability to feel anything
is nowhere to be found.

92) Never Meant to Be

I try to enter your heart
but the door is locked
ive tried every key
for hours I knocked.

It must be made of stone I conclude
and decide to break it down
thrashing the barrier with a hammer
I look like a clown

I tried to light it on fire
but the door remains the same
I hit it till my fists burn
even try to magic it open with my name

at last, I am defeated
on the ground I sit
maybe the door didn't open
because I was never meant to enter it.

93) Ineffable

A dream beyond my grasp, a star too far way
Love that's unattainable, a friendship never meant to stay
The peace I desire, the happiness I crave
out in the distance, like a tumbling wave

The ambition I still chase, the success I need
Time that remains elusive, the closure I seek
The sand slipping through my fingers, the wind blowing away
Memories that fade over time, remembrances that play

The truth we strive for, the hope that never dies
The vast knowledge, a secret full of lies
A shadow of a fantasy, that's always near
a longing that will never disappear

The desperation and yearning for each
things that will always be out of my reach.

94) Words

words
their allure consumes me
as they hold me up
and throw me in the sea
but as I drown
I can only think about their beauty
and my want for more
I might be submerged
but I am free
I take in a deep breath
the water fills my lungs
but I can breathe
better than ever before.

95) Last

life
wont always be great
but at least I will always
I poetry to write.

96) My Heart, a Sacred Temple; who I am

3 months ago, I wrote you a list
(the beginning of my future commentary)
I acknowledged who you truly were
I didn't call you by any other name
I let you know the true nature of your heart
that it was cruel
that it convinced me evil exists
that angry people make people angry
and monsters don't always know they're monsters.

But contagion is an interesting thing
after you burned down our house that I created brick by brick
and accused me of lighting it on fire
with burnt out cigarettes that you had placed in my hands
You called me a manipulative hypocrite (??)
and other cold words
You told me you don't know who I am

But I know who I am

I love tulips
I buy dim sums every time my mom
yells at me
I love wordsearches and the smell of

worn out books that make you want to choke
and if you asked my 7-year-old sister
what comes to her mind when she thinks of me
she'd say
fairy blush.

I'm sensitive
I'm kind
I'm loyal
I can also rhyme.

I can do anything
Anything
even forget about you.

Because my heart is a temple in repair now
where angels I created stay
and sing me poetry about love and respect
with fresh flowers from my garden
in their soft hands
The longer they stay here
the more I am sure
that the more I step into becoming a poet
the less I fall into liking you
The more I step into my poetry
the more I forget about you
 (demons and all)

The more I step into being a poet
the more I forget about you.

Haiku's

1) Fragmented
   I stare at the glass
   it lies shattered on the floor
   she stares back at me.

2) Moongazing
   I look at the moon
   and hope that from where you are
   you look at it too.

3) Loathe
   My nails, blunt yet sharp
   scratch at my arms and thighs till
   I bleed pink all over.

4) Hi
   Sadness is alive
   she lives in the house next door
   I feel her presence.

5) Comfort
   I missed you today
   when the rain hit heavily
   no one held my hand.

6) Poetry
   I found peace in pain
   with a pen and old notebook
   called it poetry.

7) To Drown
   I missed you in waves
   big, blue ones that crash loudly
   never thought I'd drown.

8) Regret
   Sorry that I left
   I only did it because
   I thought you would first.

9) Teenagers
   As a punishment
   I thought God would torture me
   being fifteen is worse.

10) Healer
    The healer on my porch
    had claimed she could set me free
    with hands on my neck.

11) New Year
    When the year is new
    and January wants to come by
    beware of her lies.

www.ingramcontent.com/pod-product-compliance
Lightning Source LLC
LaVergne TN
LVHW041852070526
838199LV00045BB/1567